A Gypsy's Journey
Who Finally Found
A Home

Melanie Kosiba

Presentation by *BookLeaf Publishing*

Web: www.bookleafpub.com

E-mail: info@bookleafpub.com

ISBN: 9789357441650

First edition 2023

*I dedicate this book to my Mom and Dad.
the two people who taught me what it meant
to fight from rock bottom, to never give up,
to never surrender and no matter what Love
always wins!*

ACKNOWLEDGEMENT

I'd like to thank everyone I've ever met along the way. You have helped me one way or anonther learn and grow. I realized i don't need to weild a sword anymore for I am the sword. I have gone from a Fighting warrior to a Peaceful warrior.

PREFACE

I wrote these poems as a way to heal from past trauma. To find myself and learn to trust t anyonehe process and love who I am as well as to help anyone who could identify with the same feelings and know that you are not alone on this journey home.A journey of losing yourself to the discovering of remembering who you are.

Innocence Lost

When I was a child I played in the dirt
No one told me or prepared me how much life
was going to hurt
I played with the fairies and collected fireflies
I wasn't ready for all the lies
Come with me to the secret garden I was told by
the man
Have some tea you may leave if you can
We"ll play a game I'm sure you'll like but never
tell
It will put you on your journey through hell
It's like hide and seek
I chose you because you were meek
So as I played the game I hid so well I forgot
who I am
I closed my eyes and went any place other than
where I was just to get away from the man
I hid amonst the dark forest trees
Buried beneanth the moonlight
I tried to stay true to myself with all my might
there was just to much for me to bare
I just gave up to the monster's stare
I lost myself the day I had to hide
for there was no one who came to seek
for the monster's prey on the weak

The Journey

I set on a path to find the girl who was lost
I promised I would find her no matter the cost
Through thick and thin
Hurricanes and volcanos
The deepest oceans i would swim
God only knows
I set forth on a journey that I had no idea what to
expect
Trials and tribulations, hardships and trauma
It wasn't all bad I also became a Mama
Now it wasn't only me on my journey but I had a
child
How was I going to do this I was still so wild
Trying to find my footing loosing ground
Before I knew it I was lost and tried turning
around
I made a choice I did not want to make as a
Mother
I gave my child up to another
Again on this journey all alone once more
It cut me like a burning sword right down to my
core
I knew the journey was about the way back to
me
No matter how difficult the terrain would be

drug abuse, domestic violence, rehab, and
overdosing is some of what i endured
on my travels along this road
sometimes it was so dark, lonely, and cold
Three son's I had to give up in order to give
them a better lifethen mine ever could of been
would I stay in hell for this sin
Then my fourth son was born during a time
when my life was at a healing point
I never had to go to the joint
I finally was in treatment to face my demons and
the monster within
I had to make peace from when it started to
begin
Forgiveness my last son, my Saving Grace
when i finally saw God's Face
Then I knew I had a choice on which path I
could take
I had a decision it was mine to make
Stay bitter and mean, resentfuland full of rage
keeping my heart locked in a cage
Or forgive and be happy, grateful loving and free
So instead of running away from myself, my
parents, my relationships, and God himself
I decided to get back on the road that leads back
to me
The long path of feeling
the inner journey of healing.

How Many Times

I thought you were the man of my dreams
Yet nothing is ever quite as it seems
Never in a million years
Did i think I'd be crying all these tears
The first time it happened
You said it was a mistake, you never meant to
slap me across the face
The second time you broke my arm
You said you didn't mean to cause any harm
The third time you whipped me with the belt
telling me this is how it should be
The Fourth time is when you finally went to far
and almost killed me

Awaken

5

Looking in the mirrior
I don't like what I see
Who is this face looking back at me
black eyes
bloody lips
it's you that I despise
Black and blues
Hidden scars
The time has come that I have to choose
Is this the life I want to live
Is this all that you have to give
Am I going to win or loose
Do I have the strength to fight
I've finally seen the light
I can stand up on my own two feet
I never knew what it means to show defeat

Guts And Glory

I thought you were the perfect man until that
dreadful day you raised your hands across my
face like a whip against the backside of a hoarse
This had to be an accident of course
Went out with the girls on friday night
Came home to you who just wanted to fight
Slam! my head went right through the glass
table
I tried to get up but wasn't capable
Sorry girls I can't go out
I just don't want to hear him argue, fuss, curse,
and shout
Here comes the I love you's and the I'm sorry's
this will never happen again
After walking on eggshells for days it has just
began
So he goes off to work
Leaves me home all alone and broke
No money, no friends, no self esteem, self
worth, no trust, no life, no desire to want to live
Yet strangely enough there is one thing he can
not take from me
My guts, the guts to walk out the door and leave
this mess all behind
For I know true Love is out there to find

Someone to love me, hold me, kiss me, let me be
who I am
First I have to find myself I know I can
I just have to look amonst the broken pieces of a
horror story
Only when i can love myself and look in the
mirror and like what I see
That's when I can say I have found the glory

Putting Out The Fuse

Be water for water flows
So flow like water and wash away everything
clean that's drowned
Gasoline also flows yet don't flow like gasoline
and burn everything to the ground
Emotions are like yin and yang
There has to be balance or you will explode like
an atomic bang
Find your darkness to your light
Make friends with your demons so you'll be
alright
Let your beautiful light shine in the dark
Don't worry child, those monsters are nothing
but bark
They can't hurt you because you learned to
forgive
send them light and learn to live
You were sent here to give them love and leave
your mark

A Hand Full Of Pills

9

It's been a month today
I can remember clearly that dreadful day
Memories flooding my heart and crashing my
soul like the waves on the ocean shore
It was as if not a single day had gone by
since the last time we said goodbye
I had a hand full of pills
you were all I could see
Yet instead of swollowing them I threw them
away
The same way you did to me

Blindsided

You listen to me but do not hear
You look at me but do not see
When you look up at the night sky do you see
the man in the moon
Is he reall there or just a reflection that will soon
disapear
Shadows dance like fairies in the pale yellow
moonlight
Loliness sings her song in the soft summer
breeze tonight
The silence cuts through the night like Raven's
claws
Opening the wounds of my heart
The scars that were once closed
The blood flowing through my veins taste
bittersweet
Yet nothing like the tears i've cried the day of
that final defeat
The fire burns a crimson red
I walk inside it with my demons that want me
dead
I am not afraid I do not fear
For I know my end is finally near
Goodbye to all the painthat will end
This broken heart I could not mend

As the burning fire consumes my demons
My spirit cries there must be a reason
See you can not kill what's inside my eyes
For the Phoenix She will rise

Our Place

I came upon an empty bench by a beautiful tree
I sat for awhile and thought about you and me
I thought about all the times we shared, the
laughter, joy, and happiness
I even thought about our first kiss
Oh, how it made my heart sing to just sit for
awhile and reminice
I sat for awhile and watched the sunset
It was at the place where we first met
I realized to everyone else it was just a bench
and a beautiful tree
Yet it will always be just for you and me

Wishing

In the darkness I sit under the moon
Wishing on a star that I'll be with you soon
Wildflowers dancing in the breeze
Dreams of you set my heart at ease
Although we're miles away
In your arms I know I'll be one day

Away

In a galagy far away is where my thoughts love
to roam
Aching for the feeling of finding my home
Somewhere lost in the milyway
It's where my dreams want to stay
Stars as bright as the eternal flame
I'm not the kind that you can tame
Flying free as a bird high in the sky
I'll see you soon, never goodbye
This is not my home I can not lie
Moonbeams on my skin
Stardust in my hair
Constelations in my eyes
It's time to live another day with a beautiful
sunrise
Let the journey home begin

Chance

Do I take the chance and open my heart
Should I take down my walls and let you in
I have no control it has already started to begin
That shimmer in your eyes
The smirk on your lips
I can't keep you at bay
I know because I tried
I'm not fighting too hard, what a surprise
The feelings inside are starting to rise
Do I take a chance and let you in
If I didn't it would be such a sin

Love Is A Verb

Always remember, It's not about who you love
It most definitely should never be about who
doesn't love you in return
Love is the fire from your soul intended to burn
Forget about how the one's you gave your heart
and soul to treated you
The truth of the matter is this
In the end there is only one thing rhat will exist
That my beloved is
How did you love while you were sent here
To be unapollogenticlly authentic in your truth
of self
Never place your heart upon a shelf
Don't live by the expectations of what others
want you to appear as they push and shove
Stand in your truth
You are Love the Angelic messenger from up
above

Balance

The sea looks at the sky and admires how much
peace she has
The sky looks at the sea and admires the strength
he shows
She adores the way in which he effortlessly
flows
Neither of them realize they are a reflection of
the other's beauty
Sometimes the sky can seem so gloomy
That's when the sea can get so stormy
Yet the sky does not look down at the sea
Nor does the sea look up at the sky and judge
They bring each other balance in the name of
Love
As above, so below
Love is all they know

Why Can't It Be

Before the beginning of time it was you and me
How can you doubt this feeling that I have for
you
Don't you believe I can be the one that was sent
to set you free
I know you have insecurities
Tell me why you don't believe
Is it because the man chases the woman
Well this is the age of a new Dawn
We're here to sing a new song
See, I've been searching for you since before the
sun
Centuries and light years before life even begun
Look within your soul you will remember
Let go of the ego it will all come back to you
The memory of Love, real and true

The Spark That Ignited Gypsyfire

I am beautiful
I am rare
I am special
I was spared
I lived a life full of anger and despair
Lost love, drugs, and never really cared
My faith was strong that there was more than
this
Yet everyday I felt like I was living in the abyss
I turned my back on God
After all he took everyone I ever loved
Why should I believe in someone from up above
Then that night came when death knocked on
my door
I begged for him so many times before
Tonight I wasn't ready to go
So I cried out to God, please No
Five more minutes and i would of been dead
That's what the EMS workers said
God had bigger plans for me instead
No longer do I drink and drug today
I try to live my life with compassion and love
each and every day
I am perfectly imperfect and that's alright by me

was given another chance to live life by
example for everyone to see

The Captain Of My Ship

The anchor is always needed to hold you down
You can definately do without the Kling-ons
They only surface when you have something
they need otherwise they never come around
We lower our anchors to secure ourselves and
throw the Kling-ons overboard to lighten the
load
The journey of life is not an easy one to endure
Yet you don't have to travel it alone
There is a beautiful sunrise over the horizon
I promise it will be an adventure for sure
For way too long we have traveled the lonely,
angry, pain filled seas
Trying to outrun the waves of depression, self
harm, hatred, addiction, and anxieties
My inner demons have me under scrutiny
Oh, but don't get it twisted
I am much meaner than my demons
I've taken their rights away but don't keep them
mistreated
They can still play
I just took away the power for them to say "
Parlay"
My demons were created by what life threw my
way to destroy me

I was created by the one's who I've loved and
lost along with their memories and qualities
I am the Captain of my ship
Always remember though every captain is
subject to Mutany

True North

I gathered all i had which was only what was on
my back
I decided to travel a path and a journey to find
out where all the things were that i lack
I use to think that I was always somewhat
incomplete
I always thought I had to compete
Be prettier, skinner, smarter, tougher, gentler,
kinder, more understanding
That's not what they wanted from me it was for
me to be more conforming
Follow the rules of society
Sorry that's not my destiny
I'm a rebel, rule breaker, truth seeker, bullshit
detector
Most of all I am a protector
That of the innocent, the victimized
Those who feel paralized
See I've been down that path
I've gone through the wrath
I've been to Hell and back
I realize there is nothing that I lack
I've been Blessed beyong compare
It was God who said my life he'll spare

Then asked me "Don't you know how beautiful
you truly are my child?"
You have a gift inside you that should never be
tamed but must stay wild
Remember that you are Love
That you come from up above
You shine as bright as a star in the night sky
So don't let your life pass you by
Remember who you are and who you were
before all the trauma
Look inside yourself past all the drama
Listen to that quiet voice that speaks softly in
your ear
You know, the one that you sometimes don't
want to hear
That is your inner compass
The Captain who will always steer
You can never get lost or stray
Just as long as it's your path that you stay
Always be you and stay true during the storms
Even when you feel tattered and worn
Never forget your worth
Only you and your inner compass will always
find your way back to your True North

Inner Fire

Where is my inner child inside
Where does she go when she is so scared and
tries to hide
What is she feeling when there is no one to
protect her and keep her safe and sound
Is she doomed to be left alone all tied up and
bpund
Well she screamed in silence
Having to endure the violence
Where does she go to feel safe and secure
Is there anyone who has a cure
The demons surround her at night
They keep her in a state of fright
All she longs longs for is her shining Knight
She sits quietly by her dragon who breathes his
fire for her light
She stays by his side so when the monsters come
she does't have to put up a fight
It's lonely for a little girl in the dark
All by herself with just a spark
She asks her dragon to guide her way
For hidden alone she can no longer stay
He takes a piece of his heart and gives it to her
so she can keep it close by her side

As she takes her journey and breaks through to
the other side
Cut, scraped, burned and almost broken
She is grateful for her dragon's love token
He watches her adjust to the light of the sun
He reminds her no matter how old she gets to
always have fun
If in the darkness she gets nerveous and does not
trust
Facing her fears is a must
The moon will illuminate the shadows of the
darkness
The light will get rid of the illussions of madness
She must never forget the gift of the dragon's
heart
It is to ignight the lost fire and make it restart

Time to Forgive And Heal

How do I forgive you and all that you have done
Once a child, my life was in ruins and
completely unspun
Never feeling wanted
Never feeling loved by you
Never feeling worthy of living since the age of
two
Lost and alone sittting in a room
My heart filled with nothing but anger, sadness,
pain, lonliness, despair and gloom
I keep my heart locked away hidden in a cage
I can't build a healthy relationship because I'm
so filled with rage
I can't feel any love at all
I've built up such a huge wall
No one to confide in
No one to trust
Just someone who lingers over me with eyes full
of lust
A child should never be touched by a man in
that way
Don't speak a word of this it's our own little
secret
How I live my life full of regret

I don't tell a soul about this, they won't believe
what I say
Lord knows that God didn't when I would pray
I keeep my silence
My life is so full of violence
I hate my life like this
I feel like I'm living in the abyss
No one even cared
Why don't you try walking a day in my shoes if
you dared
Oh yeah and the one person I loved most in the
world and could do no wrong
God took from me and now he's singing an
angel's song
Daddy why did you have to go and die
My soul is broken my spirit can only cry
Mommy help me I'm so scared inside
Oh that's right the needle took your life and you
died
Instead of just beating, yelling and not wanting
to see
Why did you not take a moment and just listen
to me
The only one who could get me out of here is
God Almighty
I'm so angry at him I turned my back on him
already
He took everyone i've ever loved and left me all
alone I hate him

I'm the one who turned my back on him and
began to sin
I don't want this life it's too painful I can't get by
I'll just keep sticking the needle in my arm
I'm so numb and continue to get high
Wait God no not yet I don't want to die
You've given me a second chance and I don't
completly understand why
Years have passed by good things have
happened to make me proud
Yet the pain in my heart beats so loud
I'm so full of rage, so full of pain, so full of
anger, so full of shame,
So full of guilt, so full of grief I feel so insane
I just want to hide
I feel so unworthy inside
No one to trust
I feel so alone
It's an emtiness that cuts right down to the bone
All I've been doing my whole life is trying to
survive
I really just want to be happy and thrive
I want to live, love, and heal
I want to be loved and happy and finally feel
I want someone special I can cherish in my life
I want to be a loving wife
I want to forgive those who wern't there and
took me for granted
I want to forgive those who left me abandoned

I'm no longer playing my life on rewind
I forgive all those who left me behind
It's time to say goodbye to family and friends of
my past
 can create new memories that will last
Even though my innocence was stolen from me
at such a cost
I have to move on from the chidhood I lost
I forgive you all for the demons you had
I understand you yourself did't know any better
So to move on and close this chapter of my life
is why i wrote this letter
It's not only about forgiving you
It's mostly about forgiving me so I can finally set
my heart free
To let the little girl inside know that she has
always been worthy

Gypsyfire's Creed

I never give up
I never give in
I keep trying and doing until I win
Yet if I should stumble and fall along the way
I will never land on my face
I will fall to my knees for i don't comprehend the
meaning of defeat
My spirit is strong and will never retreat
I am blessed with the power of God's Grace